CASTLES OF
SCOTLAND

THE FEUDALISATION OF SCOTLAND

Though feudal institutions were introduced into England after the Norman Conquest in 1066, and the fortified residences of the feudal lords became an integral part of the English countryside, it was not until the 12th century and the reigns of Alexander I (1107–24) and more particularly his brother David I (1124–53) that feudal land tenure and castles came to lowland Scotland.

The death of Alexander and David's father, Malcolm Canmore, in 1093 had led to turmoil in Scotland and they had sought refuge in England, where they grew up in the feudal world of the Norman court. The effect was evidently greatest on David, who returned to Scotland and began to introduce Norman retainers, feudal landholding and earth and timber castles, and greatly expanded the process when he succeeded his brother as king in 1124.

During the course of the 12th century two categories of castle were introduced into Scotland: royal castles and those built by tenants of the Crown who held their land in return for military service.

ABOVE: King David I and his grandson Malcolm IV. David introduced Norman methods of government and became the most powerful 12th-century Scottish king.

THE ANGLO-SCOTTISH WARS

The earliest stone castles were built in the mid-12th century, but it was not until the 13th century that they became common, many being constructed with curtain walls. They were built primarily as residences for their lords, but had to be available for the use of visiting monarchs. As the century progressed, the security of these castles was upgraded. Large towers were built in the angles of the curtain walls, and defensive gatehouses were added, usually consisting of pairs of massive towers with draw-bridges and portcullises.

From 1296 Edward I, having already crushed Wales, exhausted his kingdom's resources in a ruthless attempt to conquer Scotland. Earning himself the title 'Hammer of the Scots', he captured all the castles in central and southern Scotland and garrisoned them with English cavalry who terrorised the surrounding districts into submission. He used his invincible cavalry squadrons to win great victories, including the Battle of Falkirk (1298) against the strong and courageous Scottish hero, William Wallace. Wallace was executed by Edward I in 1305, but in the following year the tenacious Robert the Bruce claimed the Scottish throne.

Edward I died in battle in 1307, leaving his great rival Bruce mismatched with his own weak and unwarlike son, Edward II. Bruce wrested control of the lowland castles from the English forces, resorting to guerrilla raids that weakened their supply lines and left their castles vulnerable to Scottish attack. His policy was then to dismantle any stronghold that might prove of strategic value to the English. In 1314 Bruce defeated Edward II's army at Bannockburn, completing his rout of the occupying forces and achieving freedom for Scotland for his lifetime. The Anglo-Scottish wars continued intermittently and usually disastrously for the Scots for centuries, and even after the Union of the Crowns in 1603, when Scotland's new king, James VI, also became king of England, there were bitter quarrels across the border.

RIGHT: King Robert I (Robert the Bruce) and his first wife Isabelle of Mar, from a late 16th-century pictorial record of the Scottish Royal Family.

THE TOWER-HOUSE

Few barons of late-medieval Scotland had either the means or the necessity to indulge in the building of major castles, and therefore they erected the less grandiose but more economic tower-houses: tall, narrow structures in which the main apartments were piled one above the other.

The earliest towers, erected during the 13th and 14th centuries, were usually of a simple rectangular plan and comprised a ground-floor cellar, the entrance and a hall at first-floor level, and one or more upper storeys. More complex structures with ancillary wings, often forming an L- or Z-shaped plan, became increasingly common as the years passed by. The walls of the earlier towers were usually bound together and strengthened by massive stone buttresses, while the later towers, built when the need for military strength had declined, were less massively constructed.

In the 16th century, when the influence of European styles became felt through the French connections of the Scottish kings, the lords sought more domestic comfort. Gradually, the tower-houses' defensive characteristics disappeared or were converted into ornamental features, and the buildings were extended horizontally, thus altering the original concept of their design. By the 17th century the tower-house, after dominating baronial residences architecturally for more than three centuries, had begun to be superseded by a new type of residence – the laird's house.

ABOVE: A scene from a medieval manuscript showing labourers constructing a tower under close supervision.

BELOW: The 14th-century Archibald's Tower at Threave Castle stands five storeys high.

Queen Victoria described Balmoral as a 'pretty little castle in the old Scottish style'.

BALMORAL

13km (8 miles) W of Ballater on A93, Aberdeenshire
Tel: 013397 42534
Owned by Her Majesty The Queen

The immense castellated mansion of Balmoral is set in the gently wooded countryside of the River Dee. Robert II had a hunting lodge here, then Sir Malcolm Drummond built a tower on the same site. In c.1845 Queen Victoria and Prince Albert paid their first visit to Balmoral. Prince Albert paid £31,500 for the 9,720-hectare (24,000-acre) estate and collaborated with an Aberdeen architect, William Smith, to create a picturesque, neo-Gothic mansion in white granite. The prince supervised every detail, including carpets and curtains, and designed a Balmoral tartan for the Royal Family's exclusive use. Queen Victoria found Balmoral a 'dear paradise' and it remains the Royal Family's favourite Scottish retreat today.

LEFT: *The royal castle of Balmoral stands in picturesque grounds on the banks of the Dee.*

BLAIR

13km (8 miles) NW of Pitlochry on
B8079, Perth & Kinross
Tel: 01796 481207
Owned by the Blair Charitable Trust

Blair Castle has undergone many
changes since it was first built
around Comyn's Tower in 1269. By
the time Mary Queen of Scots stayed
here in 1564, this early tower had
been extended to include a
great hall.

During the Civil War, the
Royalist castle was captured
by Cromwell's troops. During
the Jacobite rebellion of
1745–6 Blair was the last
private castle in Britain to be
besieged when Lord George
Murray, who had forfeited his
inheritance by supporting
Bonnie Prince Charlie, laid
siege to his own home. By
1758 the castle had been remodelled as a Georgian
mansion, but in 1869 the architect Sir David Bryce
restored the medieval appearance. Blair has an impressive
collection of Sèvres porcelain, Chippendale and Sheraton
furniture, and Holbein, Lely and de Witt family portraits.

ABOVE AND RIGHT: **The last private castle to
be besieged in Britain, Blair Castle is today a
sumptuous stately home, furnished with
treasures and relics from many centuries.**

BRAEMAR

1km (½ mile) N of Braemar on A93, Aberdeenshire
Tel: 01339 741 219
Owned by Captain A.A.C. Farquharson, MC of Invercauld

Braemar Castle was originally built by John Erskine, Earl of Mar, in
1628 when he commissioned the L-shaped tower-house. The property
was burned out by the enemy clan leader John Farquharson after the
Jacobite uprising of 1689.

In 1748, two years after the devastating defeat of the clans at Culloden,
Braemar Castle was rebuilt to accommodate English soldiers, names of
whom can still be seen carved in the wooden casements. The remarkable
star-shaped curtain wall was added so that all angles could be covered by
the garrison firing through the many gun-loops.

LEFT: **The 17th-century castle at Braemar stands within
a star-shaped curtain wall with many gun-loops.**

BRODICK

On the Isle of Arran, N Ayrshire
Tel: 01770 302202
Owned by The National Trust for Scotland

Situated on the northern shore of Brodick Bay on the beautiful Isle of Arran, Brodick Castle was the seat of the Dukes of Hamilton and latterly the Duke of Montrose until 1958, when it passed to The National Trust for Scotland. Built on the site of a Viking stronghold, the castle dates in part from the 13th century, but was extended in 1652 by Oliver Cromwell, and greatly extended and renovated in sumptuous style in 1844.

There are paintings to be seen from the famous Beckford and Hamilton collections as well as magnificent silver and porcelain, and the drawing room has a rich plaster ceiling with various coats of arms.

The grounds have been designated a country park and include woodland, waterfalls, trails and a magnificent walled garden in Victorian style.

ABOVE: It was to Brodick Castle, on the Isle of Arran, that Robert the Bruce fled after his defeat at Methven in 1306.

RIGHT: A coat of arms from the drawing room ceiling at Brodick.

BRODIE

7km (4½ miles) W of Forres off A96, Moray
Tel: 01309 641371
Owned by The National Trust for Scotland

Land was first given to the Brodies around 1160 by Malcolm IV but the present building was not begun until around 1560. In the early 17th century the west wing was built, but during the Civil War in 1645 the estate was attacked by Royalists. The house was only partially damaged and remained largely unchanged on the outside until the first half of the 19th century when the 22nd Brodie of Brodie decided to enlarge the house. The surrounding parkland is carpeted in spring with daffodils, many of which were bred here by Ian, 24th Brodie of Brodie.

Brodie Castle contains fine furniture, porcelain and a major art collection comprising 17th-century Dutch and early 20th-century paintings, English watercolours and works by Scottish colourists.

BELOW: Brodie Castle is a good example of the Scottish fortified house in the 16th century.

CAERLAVEROCK

13km (8 miles) SE of Dumfries on B725,
Dumfries & Galloway
Tel: 01387 770244
In the care of Historic Scotland

Built by the Maxwells, Caerlaverock Castle is
one of the best surviving examples of medieval
castle building. Edward I besieged and captured
the existing castle, built c.1280, during his
Scottish campaign of 1300. He entrusted it to
Sir Eustace Maxwell who, in 1313, declared for
Robert the Bruce rather than for Edward II, then
dismantled the castle in order that it could not
be occupied again by the English. However,
much of the original masonry and most of the
excellent gatehouse survived. The splendid east
range, with its fine Renaissance façade, was
added in the 1630s, but the castle was captured
and dismantled by the Covenanters (Scottish
Presbyterians opposed to the introduction of a
new Prayer Book by Charles I) in 1640.

*Caerlaverock, triangular in
plan, is one of Scotland's
most attractive castles.*

CASTLE FRASER

26km (16 miles) W of Aberdeen
off B944, Aberdeenshire
Tel: 0844 4932164
Owned by The National Trust
for Scotland

Building of Castle Fraser began
in about 1575 for the 6th Laird,
Michael Fraser, and was completed
in 1636. A round, seven-storey
tower and extensions were added
to the earlier keep, making this
one of the finest examples of
the Z-shaped plan.

ABOVE AND RIGHT: Castle Fraser is the
largest, most elaborate Scottish castle
built on the traditional Z-plan.

LEFT: Cawdor Castle is most famous for its involve-
ment in Shakespeare's Macbeth. The powerful
central tower is the earliest part of the castle and
dates from the 14th century.

RIGHT: *Crathes Castle was begun in the mid-16th century, when the need for military strength had declined and builders were free to concentrate on the aesthetics of their work.*

CAWDOR

9km (5½ miles) SW of Nairn on B9090, Highland
Tel: 01667 404401
Owned by the Dowager Countess Cawdor

Cawdor Castle is famous for its associations with Shakespeare's *Macbeth*. The Thanedom of Cawdor was promised to Macbeth by the witches, and people like to imagine that the castle was the setting for the murder of Duncan. However, none of the castle dates from Macbeth's time in the middle of the 11th century.

In 1454 King James II of Scotland granted a licence to the Thane of Cawdor, permitting him to fortify the five-storey tower, built around 1370, 'with walls and ditches and equip the summit with turrets and means of defence, with warlike provisions and strengths'. There was an added condition that the castle must always be ready for use by the King and his successors. This central tower is surrounded by buildings from the 17th century, which were enlarged and remodelled during the following century.

CRATHES

5km (3 miles) E of Banchory on A93, Aberdeenshire
Tel: 0844 4932166
Owned by The National Trust for Scotland

This area north of the River Dee was known as the Lands of Leys and, together with the Horn of Leys (a jewelled ivory horn now located in the main hall of the castle), was granted to Alexander Burnett by Robert the Bruce in 1323. The castle was built between 1553 and 1596 and displays many of the best features of the Scottish tower-house.

Crathes is L-shaped with many decorative turrets and dormer windows. It is well known for the quality of its painted ceilings in the Muses Room, the supposedly haunted Green Lady's Room and, most spectacularly, the Room of the Nine Nobles. The Gallery has an oak-panelled ceiling with heraldic carvings unique in Scotland.

The walled gardens contain an outstanding collection of trees and shrubs, with topiary yew hedges, parts of which date from 1702. There are six woodland walks.

*The magnificent Culzean Castle is one of
Robert Adam's most outstanding achievements.*

CULZEAN

19km (12 miles) S of Ayr on A719, S Ayrshire
Tel: 0844 4932149
Owned by The National Trust for Scotland

Culzean Castle was built by Robert Adam for the Kennedy family between 1777 and 1792,
replacing an earlier tower-house. Built in an ostentatiously Italianate style, Culzean is an
impressive structure. Of particular interest are the magnificent oval staircase, the round saloon
and the plaster ceilings now restored to Adam's original colouring.

The grounds, declared Scotland's first country park in 1969, contain many features of
interest, including a deer park, swan pond and ice house, a unique pagoda, a large Victorian
vinery and an adventure playground.

DIRLETON

5km (3 miles) W of North Berwick on A198, E Lothian
Tel: 01620 850330
In the care of Historic Scotland

In the 12th century the Anglo-Norman family of de Vaux acquired the barony of Dirleton and they built the original stone castle. It was one of the most formidable Scottish castles of its time and was believed to be impervious to the stone-throwing siege engines of the 13th century. Nevertheless Bishop Anthony Bek of Durham successfully besieged the castle in 1298. The English held it until 1311 when it was recovered by the army of Robert the Bruce who probably dismantled parts of the fabric to prevent further occupation. In the mid-14th century the castle passed to the Halyburton family, who repaired and extended the buildings to include the vaults, great hall and remodelled entrance. From 1515 the Ruthven family were equally energetic in adding to the castle's buildings. In 1650 Cromwell's troops occupied and ruined the castle.

BELOW: *Dirleton Castle has seen many additions since it was first constructed in the 12th century, but has been in ruins since Cromwell's troops ransacked it in 1650.*

DOUNE

Just E of Doune on A84, Stirling
Tel: 01786 841742
In the care of Historic Scotland

Doune Castle is one of the largest and best-preserved examples of 14th-century castle architecture in Scotland. Comprising a powerful curtain wall enclosing a large court dominated by the square gatehouse-tower, it was built in a highly strategic position on an elevated promontory of land. The triangular site is naturally well defended, being protected on two sides by the Rivers Teith and Ardoch, and on the third by a deep ditch. In the 15th and 16th centuries, Doune was used as a royal retreat and hunting lodge by successive monarchs. Within its buildings are many rooms, passageways and fine halls.

RIGHT: The 14th-century castle at Doune occupies a triangular site and is dominated by the gatehouse-tower.

DRUM

16km (10 miles) W of Aberdeen off A93, Aberdeenshire
Tel: 0844 4932161
Owned by The National Trust for Scotland

Drum's powerful square tower-house, one of the three oldest surviving in Scotland, was built in the late 13th century. In 1323 Drum was granted by Robert the Bruce to his faithful standard-bearer, William de Irwyn, and it remained in the possession of the Irvine family until 1976 when it was bequeathed to The National Trust for Scotland. The tower now stands as one side of a courtyard; in 1619 the 9th Laird added the very impressive Renaissance mansion.

The extensive grounds include woodland walks and a garden of historic roses.

LEFT: The powerful 13th-century tower at Drum dominates the 1619 mansion.

DRUMLANRIG

5km (3 miles) N of Thornhill off A76,
Dumfries & Galloway
Tel: 01848 331555
Owned by the Duke of Buccleuch and
Queensberry, KT

The present castle was constructed
between 1679 and 1691 by
William Douglas, 1st Duke of
Queensberry, on the site of a
previous Douglas stronghold. Built
in local pink sandstone, it is a fine
example of Scottish domestic
architecture. The castle has associations with Robert the Bruce, Mary
Queen of Scots and Robert Burns,
and houses a renowned art collection, including works by da Vinci,
Rembrandt, Holbein, Kneller and
Ramsay. The beautiful French
furniture includes two cabinets
presented by Louis XIV to
Charles II.

BELOW: *Deep in the beautiful Nithsdale area
of south-west Scotland lies Drumlanrig
Castle, the 17th-century home of the Dukes
of Buccleuch and Queensberry.*

The massive Clan Maclean stronghold of Duart Castle appears to rise out of the cliffs of Duart Bay on the Isle of Mull.

DUART

Just E of Lochdon on the Isle of Mull,
Argyll & Bute
Tel: 01680 812309
Owned by Sir Lachlan Maclean, Bt

Duart Castle stands on a rocky promontory called *Dubh Ard*, meaning Black Point. The keep at Duart dates from the 13th century and parts of the original enclosing wall survive. It has always been the home of the Macleans with one short break, in the aftermath of Culloden, when it was garrisoned by the English. In 1911 Sir Fitzroy Maclean repurchased and restored the castle; it is now lived in by the present chief, Sir Lachlan Maclean.

DUNROBIN

2.5km (1½ miles) NE of Golspie on A9, Highland
Tel: 01408 633177
Owned by the Sutherland Trust

The ancestral seat of the Dukes and Earls of Sutherland, Dunrobin was originally built in the late 13th century by Robert, 2nd Earl of Sutherland. It was dominated by the massive square keep, which survives today. Sir Charles Barry, the architect of the Houses of Parliament, completely redesigned the castle during the period 1835–50, creating a highly imaginative baronial residence. In 1915, while in use as a naval hospital, the castle was badly damaged by fire, but it was subsequently restored to Barry's design by Sir Robert Lorimer who also contributed a library and several new rooms.

Dunrobin Castle, with its 189 rooms, was used for seven years in the mid-20th century as a boys' boarding school. The castle contains a fine collection of paintings, furniture and tapestries, and the magnificent formal gardens are retained in their original Victorian design.

DUNVEGAN

Just N of Dunvegan on the A850, Isle of Skye, Highland
Tel: 01470 521206
Owned by John MacLeod of MacLeod

Dunvegan Castle has been the ancestral seat of the MacLeods of MacLeod for nearly 800 years and still remains their home. The Fairy Tower, the old curtain wall, the dungeon and the original sea-gate (at one time the only entrance) are remnants of earlier centuries of MacLeod building. However, the extensive work that was undertaken during the 17th, 18th and 19th centuries tends to mask the castle's original medieval appearance.

Some interesting relics are displayed, including the celebrated Fairy Flag, the Dunvegan Cup, Rory Mor's Horn and a lock of Bonnie Prince Charlie's hair.

ABOVE: *The famous seat of the Clan MacLeod, Dunvegan Castle lies in the north-west corner of the Isle of Skye.*

LEFT: *Dunrobin Castle, the ancestral home of the Dukes and Earls of Sutherland, stands majestically on a natural terrace overlooking Dornoch Firth in the Highlands.*

LEFT: *The tiny Romanesque St Margaret's Chapel was built by David I in honour of his mother, Queen Margaret. It is the oldest building in Edinburgh.*

EDINBURGH

In the centre of Edinburgh
Tel: 0131 225 9846
In the care of Historic Scotland

Edinburgh Castle stands 135m (443ft) above sea level on a plug of volcanic rock. The buildings range in date from the 12th-century St Margaret's Chapel to the 20th-century Scottish National War Memorial. It is known that the site was fortified in the Iron Age but it entered historical records in the reign of Malcolm Canmore (1058–93) who made Edinburgh one of his principal residences. His wife, Margaret, became renowned for her piety and charity and was later canonised. The little chapel that bears her name has stood on the rock through nearly eight and a half centuries of Scottish history. Margaret died in the castle in November 1093, after hearing of the death in battle of her husband and her eldest son.

The castle was captured in 1314 by the Scottish army led by the Earl of Moray, nephew of Robert the Bruce. With only 30 men, Moray scaled the rock and the walls at midnight, overpowered the English garrison and took the castle.

Time and again, as the Anglo-Scottish wars persisted, Edinburgh changed hands. It suffered considerable damage, but repairs and alterations were continually being carried out. Today only the ruin of David's Tower dates from the defences built before the 15th century. The subsequent rebuilding of the 16th and 17th centuries concentrated on the residential aspects of the castle. This is clearly seen in the main buildings, such as the palace and the great hall.

Edinburgh Castle is Scotland's greatest tourist attraction, offering fascinating insights and superb views of the city and beyond.

ABOVE: The spectacular Military Tattoo is held on the floodlit Castle Esplanade during the Edinburgh Festival each summer.

BELOW: Edinburgh Castle's famous 15th-century artillery piece 'Mons Meg' was used at the siege of the English castle of Norham (1497), but in 1681 burst while firing a salute.

The dramatic and imposing castle site at Edinburgh has probably been fortified since the Iron Age, though the present buildings date from the reign of Malcolm Canmore (1058–93).

Yet Edinburgh castle still retained an importance as a military stronghold. The powerful approach to its heart, beneath Half Moon Battery and through Portcullis Gate, was constructed in the late 16th century. During the Civil War the castle surrendered to Cromwell after a three-month bombardment in 1650. It surrendered again in 1689, this time to William of Orange after holding out for the last Stuart king, James II (VII of Scotland). The final defence was in 1745, when Bonnie Prince Charlie, marching south with his Highlanders to the Battle of Prestonpans, occupied Edinburgh for 40 days. They blockaded the castle, but soon realised they could not take it. Within a year many of them found themselves prisoners there following the collapse of their cause at the bloody Battle of Culloden. Since then Edinburgh Castle, indeed Scotland, has rested at peace.

The castle became a prison for French soldiers during the Napoleonic wars. Since then many British monarchs have visited this famous site of so much of Scotland's dramatic history and, fittingly, the castle was chosen to enshrine the Scottish National War Memorial in the wake of the First World War.

EILEAN DONAN

Just S of Dornie on A87, Highland
Tel: 01599 555202
Owned by The Conchra Charitable Trust

Standing on a rocky island at the junction of three lochs and linked to the mainland by a causeway, Eilean Donan originated in 1220 as one of Alexander II's defences against the Danes. It was held by the Jacobites in 1719 and heavily bombarded by an English warship. The castle remained a ruin until 1932 when Colonel MacRae-Gilstrap restored it to its former condition.

The magnificent 13th-century castle of Eilean Donan stands on an island at the junction of Lochs Long, Duich and Alsh.

Floors Castle is a stately home with magnificent rooms that are open to the public.

FLOORS

2km (1 mile) NW of Kelso on A6089, Borders
Tel: 01573 223333
Owned by the Duke of Roxburghe

The ancestral seat of the Dukes of Roxburghe, Floors Castle was built by Robert Adam's father, William, in the years 1721–5. This renowned family of Scottish-born architects built in a style that was basically Roman and Italian rather than native. However, Floors was extended and given most of its present appearance by William Playfair in the middle of the 19th century.

Floors is said to be the largest inhabited mansion in Scotland and contains splendid furnishings, tapestries and paintings. In the grounds a holly tree marks the spot where Scotland lost James II, one of her more able kings. A great enthusiast for artillery, he stood too close to one of his cannons when it exploded during the siege of the English-held Roxburgh Castle in 1460.

FYVIE

13km (8 miles) S of Turriff off A947, Aberdeenshire
Tel: 0844 4932182
Owned by The National Trust for Scotland

Dating from the 13th century but built on the site of a royal stronghold, this stately castellated mansion is a superb example of Scottish Baronial architecture. Each of Fyvie's five towers is supposed to have been built by one of the five families that have owned it.

The castle's opulent interior includes the outstanding Wheel Stairway and fine collections of portraits, tapestries, arms and armour. In the landscaped grounds are lochside walks, a walled fruit and vegetable garden and a restored racquets court.

RIGHT: **The many ghost stories and legends associated with Fyvie give the castle an air of mystery.**

LEFT: *Glamis Castle was the childhood home of Queen Elizabeth the Queen Mother, and Princess Margaret was born here in 1930.*

GLAMIS

8km (5 miles) W of Forfar off A94, Angus
Tel: 01307 840393
Owned by the Earl of Strathmore and Kinghorne

Glamis Castle is the imposing and historic home of the earls of Strathmore and Kinghorne. The castle owes its present appearance, with its numerous turrets and battlements, to the 17th century. However, parts of the L-shaped tower date from the 15th century. When Lady Glamis was burned for witchcraft and conspiracy to murder James V in 1537, the castle was forfeited to the Crown, though when her innocence had been established it was restored to her son, and the Strathmore family has held it ever since.

Today the castle, with its close ties to the Royal Family, is a popular tourist attraction. There is much to see in the castle and grounds. Of note are Duncan's Hall, the oldest part of the castle, and King Malcolm's Room, traditionally believed to be the place of the King's death. The grounds include a late 19th-century formal garden and an Italianate garden.

RIGHT: *The Great Hall at Glamis dates largely from the 17th century, when the castle was remodelled by the Earls of Strathmore and Kinghorne to create a larger and more comfortable family home.*

HERMITAGE

Just W of Hermitage on B6399, Borders
Tel: 01387 376222
In the care of Historic Scotland

Known to have been in existence in the late 13th century, Hermitage Castle was repaired by Edward I in 1300 at a cost of £20. This brooding castle was the scene of many violent feuds and border skirmishes.

The earliest parts of the present H-shaped building have been dated to the middle of the 14th century. Mary Queen of Scots made her historic ride from Jedburgh to Hermitage when her lover, the Earl of Bothwell, lay wounded in the castle in 1566, a round trip of approximately 88km (55 miles) over the hills in mid-October. By the 18th century the castle was in ruins, but was extensively repaired by the Duke of Buccleuch in 1820.

ABOVE: The bleak border stronghold of Hermitage Castle still conveys an air of massive impregnability.

RIGHT: Mary Queen of Scots (1542–67).

HUNTLY

At Huntly on A96, Aberdeenshire
Tel: 01466 793191
In the care of Historic Scotland

In the late 12th century, Duncan, Earl of Fife, built a castle on this well-protected site. It was known as the Peel of Strathbogie. During the reign of Robert the Bruce the castle was confiscated and given to Sir Adam Gordon of Huntly, Berwickshire, but the castle was not renamed until 1544. The imposing ruins of the Renaissance palace built between 1597 and 1602 now dominate the castle complex.

LEFT: Huntly Castle's fine example of tower-house construction dates from the end of the 16th century.

The fine Gothic-style façade of Inveraray Castle conceals magnificently decorated Georgian rooms.

INVERARAY

At Inveraray, Argyll & Bute
Tel: 01499 302203
Owned by the Trustees of the 10th Duke of Argyll

The seat of the Duke of Argyll, head of Clan Campbell, Inveraray Castle is situated on the north-west border of Loch Fyne amidst some of the finest highland scenery. The old castle, built by Colin Campbell in about 1415 close to the site of the present castle, was swept away, as was the nearby town, in the grand scheme of rebuilding carried out by Roger Morris and Robert Mylne in the middle of the 18th century for the 3rd and 5th Dukes.

The castle is built of locally quarried blue-grey chlorite schist. It is one of the earliest examples of Gothic revival architecture, the garden front being the most complete and attractive example of the style. The medieval character was achieved through the round towers, the lance-headed windows and arches, the decorative stone palisading and the central tower, built in the style of a baronial keep.

The castle houses an outstanding collection of furniture, paintings and porcelain, and some interesting early Scottish weapons. After fire damage to the roof in the 1870s, the corner towers were topped with tall conical slate roofs.

KILCHURN

2km (1 mile) W of Dalmally on A85,
Argyll & Bute
Tel: 01786 431 326
In the care of Historic Scotland

Situated in a picturesque setting at
the head of Loch Awe, Kilchurn
Castle was built by Colin Campbell
in about 1450 as a rectangular
tower. It was substantially altered in
1693 to provide barracks accom-
modation for the earl's private
army. The rocky spit on which the
castle stands was an island until
1817, when the level of the loch
was lowered.

BELOW: Kilchurn Castle was abandoned after
it was struck by lightning in the 1760s, but
is now being consolidated and repaired.

LEFT AND ABOVE: The rocky-looking ruined
castle of St Andrews dates chiefly from
the 16th century, though the site has been
fortified since c.1200.

ST ANDREWS

In St Andrews on A91, Fife
Tel: 01334 477196
In the care of Historic Scotland

St Andrews Castle occupies a coastal promontory and is protected on the north and east by the cliffs and sea. It was cut off on the south and west sides by a deep ditch, the approach to the entrance being by a drawbridge. The castle as it survives today is principally the work of the 14th and 16th centuries, but it incorporates within its walls parts of earlier work. The original castle was built c.1200 by Bishop Roger.

During the Wars of Independence the castle was captured, recaptured, dismantled and rebuilt by both sides until, in 1337, it was recaptured by Sir Andrew Moray who dismantled it to avoid the risk of it falling under English control again. For about fifty years the castle lay in ruins until it was rebuilt by Bishop Walter Traill.

The castle's most turbulent associations are with Cardinal David Beaton (1539–46), a man of strong Catholic ambitions who had the Protestant reformer George Wishart burnt to death for heresy in 1546. The cardinal was himself murdered three months later by a band of Protestants, and his body then hung from a wall-head. The Protestants, with John Knox as their chaplain, were subsequently besieged in the castle for a year until the arrival of a French fleet forced them to surrender. They were taken away by the French and Knox spent the next two years as a galley slave. A feature surviving from the siege of 1546–7 is the mine and counter-mine tunnelled through the rock beneath the castle. Discovering that the besiegers were driving a tunnel with the intention of breaching the fortifications in several places, the defenders drove a number of shafts of their own until they succeeded in breaking through to the attackers' tunnel.

STIRLING

In Stirling
Tel: 01786 450000
In the care of Historic Scotland

The commanding heights of Stirling Castle dominate the main ford of the Forth, the strategic link between northern and southern Scotland. The castle has appropriately been called the 'key to Scotland', and its possession has been the focus of contention for many centuries, with battles like Stirling Bridge (1297) and Bannockburn (1314) being fought in its shadow.

The castle dates mainly from the 15th and 16th centuries when it was a principal royal residence, seeing the birth of James III, the childhood of James V and the crowning of the infant Mary Queen of Scots. Work in the 16th century largely shaped the structure as it survives today. Its main features are the central turreted gatehouse with its flanking towers and curtain wall, the Great Hall, the Palace and the Chapel Royal.

ABOVE AND TOP: The present Stirling Castle dates mainly from the 15th and 16th centuries. The original castle was dismantled by Robert the Bruce after his victory at the Battle of Bannockburn (1314).

TANTALLON

5km (3 miles) E of North Berwick off A198, E Lothian
Tel: 01620 892727
In the care of Historic Scotland

The castle stands on a dramatic promontory opposite Bass Rock. The vulnerable landward side is defended by a series of outworks and the powerful curtain wall, with an imposing cylindrical tower at each end and the gatehouse in the middle. The 14th-century castle was built by William, the 1st Earl of Douglas.

THREAVE

5km (3 miles) W of Castle Douglas off A75,
Dumfries & Galloway
Tel: 07711 223101
In the care of Historic Scotland

This 14th-century Douglas stronghold stands on an island in the River Dee. It was built by Archibald the Grim and is dominated by Archibald's Tower, which stands five storeys high. The large corbel projecting from the battlements was, by tradition, used by Archibald to hang his many victims, but in fact supported a machicolated platform defending the entrance beneath.

The strong outer curtain wall with its four cylindrical towers, each containing gun-loops, probably dates from 1455 when the castle endured its first long siege. James II was determined to destroy the Black Douglases, and in 1452 murdered the 8th Earl. The 9th Earl raised 40,000 men against James, but the Douglases were defeated at Arkinholm in 1455. As his other strongholds fell, the 9th Earl granted Threave to the English king in a desperate attempt to save it, but James was not going to be denied. He bombarded Threave without success and eventually had to bribe the garrison into surrendering. The castle was captured and dismantled by the Covenanters in 1640.

BELOW: The old Douglas stronghold of Threave is set in a picturesque site on a small island in the River Dee, and is reached by a boat that is summoned by a brass bell.

URQUHART

At Strone on A82, Highland
Tel: 01456 450551
In the care of Historic Scotland

Castle Urquhart, standing 13m (44ft) above the level of Loch Ness on a rocky promontory, is a favourite haunt for would-be spotters of the famous Loch Ness Monster. The site has revealed traces of Iron Age habitation and was probably fortified as early as the 6th century when St Columba visited the area and apparently encountered a sea creature. The original castle was built by the Durwards in the 13th century, but the ruins that survive today are largely those of the castle as it was rebuilt in the 16th and 17th centuries by the Grant family. In 1692 the castle was blown up by the troops who had occupied it after the Jacobite uprising of 1689, thus preventing it from becoming a Jacobite base at a later date. Since then it has not been occupied. In 1715 a storm blew down the south wall of the already dilapidated 16th-century tower.

LEFT: Urquhart Castle is an ideal site for 'monster spotting', occupying a rocky promontory on the northern bank of Loch Ness.

BACK COVER (inset): The gallery at Fyvie Castle was built as a ballroom and music room by Lord Leith in 1900. (background): The head of Loch Awe.

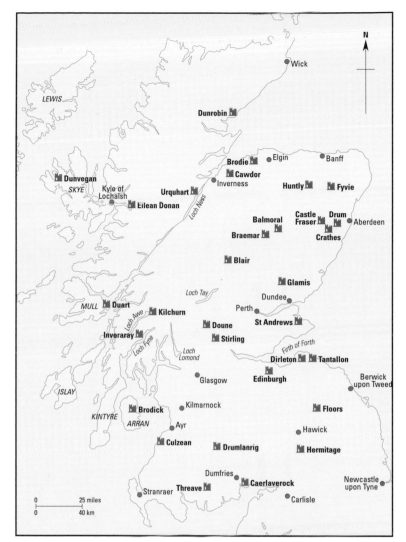

Acknowledgements

Photography by: The Blairs Museum: 22 middle; British Library: 3 top; Michael Caldwell: 24–25 bottom, back cover background; John Cleare: 14–15 top, 19 top, 22 top; Douglas Corrance: 9 inset, 10–11 top, 21 top, 26 bottom, back cover inset; Malcolm Fife: 18 top; Derek Forss: 5 top; V. K. Guy Ltd: front cover, 7, 17 top right, 23, 24 top; Historic Scotland (Crown Copyright): 16 inset, 17 bottom right; National Library of Scotland: 2 top (© Duke of Roxburghe), 2–3 bottom (© Sir David Ogilvy); Scotland in Focus (D. Barnes: ifc-1, 6 bottom/D. Burrows: 6 middle/J. Byers: 4 top, 13 bottom/P. Davies: 20 top/A.G. Firth: 6 top, 10, 27 bottom/D. Kerr: 24 middle/Bob Lawson: 11 bottom/R.M. 19 bottom, 26 top/D. McKinnell: 27 middle/G. Satterley: 21 bottom/R. Schofield: 8 top, 22 bottom/J. Smith: 8–9 top, 12 bottom/J. Weir: 14–15 bottom/R. Weir: 4–5 bottom, 5 middle, 8 bottom, 12–13 top, 14 inset, 27 top/Willbir: 18 bottom); Mick Sharp: 3 bottom, 15 right; The National Trust for Scotland (Douglas MacGregor: 20–21 bottom/David Robertson: 9 top); Stephen Whitehorne: 4 bottom left; Andy Williams: 16–17, 28.

The publishers would like to thank the administrators of the castles included for their assistance in the preparation of this guide.
Based on a text by David Cook.
Edited by Vivien Brett.
Designed by John Buckley.
Map by the Map Studio Ltd, Romsey, Hants.

Publication in this form © Pitkin Publishing Ltd 2002, latest reprint 2008.

Printed in Great Britain.
ISBN 978 1 84165 046 3   3/08

PITKIN

ISBN 978-1-84165-046-3